Cover design by: Zacharia G

Printed in the United States of America

Disclaimer:

The information contained herein has been accumulated from intense research and from real life experience. The people and names mentioned herein is used as a means of information and it is not intended to offend or disrepute any individual or company. It is the sole discretion of the reader to use the information or discard it.

AF392499

A Quick Guide

To

EASY

MONEY

Table Of Contents

Introduction

If you are here, you are in dire need of some cash, right? You may need it for some hospital procedure, or to buy your own home, or perhaps you may want it to just lead a fabulous glamorous lifestyle? You may be tired of being bombarded by e-mails and advertisements, promising great returns, but you receive **NO MONEY**, only more invitations to **sign-up** to THIS and **sign-up** to THAT!! Maybe you have a little savings tucked away and you want to invest it into something and make really huge profits, very quickly, but you don't know where to start? Its frustrating to read long pages of boring information and that is why I decided to come to *YOUR ASSISTANCE* and give you a little booklet with a *QUICK* *and EASY* way to reach your goals, or should I rather say, *TREASURES*…

So, you are familiar with names such as *Jeff Bezos*, *Elon Musk* and the *Kardashian-Jenner's*, correct? And more than their fame, you are interested in their financial statuses, not so? Let's fast forward and introduce you to some business models which are blasting all over the internet and social media platforms.

Business Module 1

CRYPTO–CURRENCY INVESTMENTS

Don't go there! If you have tried this, and it worked for you, then you wouldn't be here right now! In 2008 the world was introduced to the famous Crypto-currencies, it became very prominent very quickly, and those who had reservations, saw a "few success stories" and bought into it. The currency showed vulnerability in that the input was usually more than the output and the sales were slow. The group then introduced marketing strategies, where many retailers accepted paying with certain Crypto-currencies as a payment option. The sales in Crypto-currencies grew and the marketing increased and the popularity found its way into pushing some of them from $22 (twenty-two dollars) per unit to over $60 000 (sixty thousand dollars) per unit. Various crypto currencies erupted around the globe and made a debut.

The marketing strategy with most of them is that you encouraged to put in a minimum investment for a few months to reap great returns and profits. Thereafter, you are shown how much you can make in just 1 week with a bigger initial investment.

Being the needy sometimes greedy human beings that we are, we tend to fall for the **big deposit, short period** - and then re-deposit for a bigger return and we spend hours online, ***"watching it grow"***. So instead of paying rent to your landlord, you decide to use it for a mini-investment, or you decide to take your month's salary or the kids school fees; I mean you're going to get 20 times the amount back in a short while, right? Wrong!! The next day or week there's a fault in the online investment system, and this lasts for a few days before panic sets in; next you see the headlines on the news which reads "xxx crypto-investors cannot access their funds"; and when "trying to locate the founders or CEO of the company, they are no-where to be found"; and your investment? It is in some foreign country being enjoyed by someone with no conscience. Then an endless amount of fraud cases are opened and investigations continue for years, while you don't know what to do next.

I am not saying that it does not work; it just works for very few people who do have the extra cash; It does work for a short while, for the sake of getting the customer base to gain popularity and grow. It is for those who are willing to risk making a profit or losing it all. It's as simple as that

Business module 2

THE ONLINE SALES AGENT

Try to access a YouTube video and there you have "Sally" (pseudonym) popping up on your screen telling you that you have to get in on her success! She poses in different holiday locations, showing you how much free time and money she has, and how little time she needs to spend working, to make all this money. Ok, I admit, I fell for this one, but being the cautious person that I am, I did not spend any money! I just wasted a fair amount of time. But this does sound good, right? The sales pitch is that you should sign up to join in a webinar to hear how you can make thousands of dollars per month on Amazon. They dilly-dally and show you a number of sales figures which they themselves or some person they introduced to this system made this far. It looks really tempting, as the figures go from approximately $124 (one hundred and twenty-four dollars) per day to approximately $3100 (three thousand one hundred dollars) per day. So, Sally speaks about getting people to author and publish books on Amazon for you, you put up your price and BAM - the money starts pouring in! The term used is ***"create mini-income streams"***.

All of a sudden, the author in me came to the fore and I wanted to start writing, and I tell my kids to pray that it works and I start dreaming about what I would do with all the money I'm going to make in the next month or two. I write, I neglect my family for the sake of a "better, wealthier, more luxurious, perfect and easy life". I publish a well-researched book, tag it at a fair price, and pay nothing to upload it. That's great! I only need about 1 million people to download my book for me to reach my goal. I spent zero and the money is going to start flowing in in a short while! What is not revealed to you, is that there is an entire process to follow, and it takes a lot of time and quite a bit of effort:

i)   The registration;
ii)   The government tax requirements;
iii)   Adjusting the manuscript to prepare it for an e-book or for paperback publishing (this takes longer than writing the actual book);
iv)   The uploading; the failed uploads, etc.;
v)   Designing a cover (there are free templates though);
vi)   The publishing; The signing up of free copies to a package so that your

book has more chance of being seen, being downloaded and being read, and this works on a royalty fee.

vii) *The continuous marketing on social media platforms so that you gain popularity (and you have to pay for this service, so it is NOT FREE).*

viii) *When your book is purchased, it takes about 60 days before the payment gets into your account.*

Then the waiting starts and I'm expecting my phone to beep with messages from my bank… Yeah right, keep on dreaming! A rude awakening sets in; that there are no immediate riches here, sorry! Instead,

I receive more marketing e-mails from Sally, using the most alluring financial terms and statements, but, in this particular e-mail I noticed that she added a document with her current income from the book sales; it is over two hundred thousand dollars! But here's the catch, the figures are broken down, and it shows that in 12 months, 830 books were authored to get to the $230 000 mark. Let us do some calculating: $230 000 divided by 830 book equals to an average of about $277 per book. It dawned on me then, that that's not much if you're the author, so this process was not going to work for me. I mean 830 books in 1 year? Who has that amount of time, when there's only 365 days in a year! And if you're getting someone to author it for you, they get a cut out of that too, so the $277 is not yours alone. Your book is sitting up there, between thousands of other books, how many people are really going to notice YOUR book? I realized at this point that Sally was nothing but a sales agent, marketing for the worlds' largest online bookstore, getting loads of people to subscribe, buy, write books, upload them and she's getting paid really well for it. Good luck to her!

I don't know about you, but to me this sounds like just another ploy and it doesn't work, well, at least not as fast and not as many hundreds of thousands are made as Sally claims. By the way, at the end of each e-mail Sally sends you, and on the webinar she invites you to, there's an explicit disclaimer, which informs you that this system does not work for everyone and that the figures they quote, are not guaranteed. Yet, the alluring e-mails keep coming in and the invitations to webinars, etc. do not end. She even plays on your emotions and calls you out as "an indecisive person which is why you are unsuccessful" - YES she stoops that low! And here's the next, not so funny, joke. It pushes us into Business Module 3.

Business Module 3

MORE MARKETING

Next, Sally from the above marketing stint, starts to introduce us to some of her friends who have also made hundreds of thousands of dollars by not working too hard or for too many hours per month. Again, we are invited to register for a webinar, but this time it's with "Alex". Since I realized that Sally was just marketing for a huge company, it was my curiosity which pushed me to register for the next webinar. Really, it was my curiosity, I wanted to know "what more is there to market?"

Some more dilly-dallying and some figures and graphs to show you how great it is working. Sales can go up to thousands of dollars per day! Alex makes over $30000 per month, and he wants to share this with you…really? My curiosity irks me, because at this point I'm wondering:

"If something works well for you and you are making tons of money, would you even share this idea with your own brother or sister? Or would you try to keep it quiet for as long as possible so that no-one interrupts your cash flowing in? I would personally keep it to myself, unless, it's a marketing gimmick, and I need as

many, mostly gullible or desperate people as possible, on this band-wagon!"

As I hate wasting time, I recorded the webinar so that I could look at it later and skip the dribbling. The business module which Alex is promoting is a software app in which your customers purchase items from you (you are selling these at a profitable price) which you are, in turn, purchasing online from Walmart and they deliver it straight to the customer. Again, it strikes me that Alex is pushing sales for Walmart, and that is the truth of his business module. He is markcting for the Company and he gets paid for it and here you are, sitting in the middle, hanging onto his words because you are really desperate for some extra cash. To top it off, you have to download his purchasing software so that you can add your profit margin – and yes, he gets a cut out of that too. I receive a few more e-mails with "free hotel stays" and "a "free 30-day watch and learn how to use Alex's business model with his software program.." but I am not falling for this.

Business Module 4

THE SOCIAL MEDIA

INFLUENCING AGENCIES

Social media influencers are those personalities who usually have a really huge following. They use their platform to advertise products or to start their own businesses.

I came across one such influencing team which looked really interesting and it appealed to me. I thought to myself:

"If I load my product on their site, and they have a following of 100 000 fans, I will be a millionaire within a week. They charge a fee of

between $49 to $199 per month for different packages. That's not a bad price at all, if I'm going to make millions in a short while."

I browse through their website which is not easy to access because I am not a member yet, but I find quite a lot of information which pleases me. They can have you signed-up and running your business within a few minutes, and you can even get a **"free trial week".** My curiosity is burning up again, "What is the catch?", let me ask a few questions first and see how perfect this business option is.

I first get to speak to a **"bot" which I hate,** but it quickly switches to a "human being".

My Question: How many customers are currently signed up on your site or do I have to do my own marketing?

Answer: Marketing is not included in our plans; you will have to do your own marketing. We recommend...blah blah and we do offer marketing training..."

Thank you. I am a bit disappointed at this point. I did not expect to have to do much; I immediately lose interest in this idea.

Basically, what is offered to you is a website, with your brand/product details and selling options, etc. and it is linked to THEIR site.

You have to do **ALL THE WORK BY YOURSELF**; you have to load all your logos, business intro, products or courses, videos, etc. Actually, you do everything - only the "website "/online area you are going to use for your business, is set up for you already. You have to learn how to use it though. The reason why this doesn't work for me is because: if you have to do your own advertising, and you work up your own following of 100 000 or more, why should you integrate *YOUR FOLLOWERS into THEIR* website? **YOU** are doing **THE HARDEST WORK** here, and then you are going to pay for it? This system may work for some people, but it does not look like it is for everyone. I can't afford $49 to $199 right now, I mean, that is the reason why I need to know *HOW TO MAKE EASY MONEY, RIGHT?* Well, we are nearly there..!

Business Module 5
THE COLD HARD TRUTH

Here we need to do some research, and some history first, before we get to the truth of it all: let's take a look at those famous people, those billionaires we see on the screen and all over the Forbes Magazine, those people whose glamorous lifestyles we wish we had..

In no particular order let us start drooling at these figures (ha-ha, I'm referring to the digits)..

Name   : Alexander Wang

Age   : 25

Fortune : Above $1 Billion. Classed as the youngest billionaire in Forbes under 30 in 2018.

Requires: Skills in technology, using artificial intelligence and selling it to huge clients like Uber, Alphabet, etc.

Name   : Kylie Jenner

Age   : 24

Fortune : $1 Billion

Requires: A famous family. Modelling contracts. Make-up/Product Creation. The actual worth of Kylie is controversial, but never-the-less, she's still doing very well with the sale of her make-up kits, and selling shares of her company to Coty for around $1.2 billion.

Name   : Jeff Bezos

Age   : 58

Fortune : $165.1 Billion

Requires: Being the founder of Amazon, which started in a garage in 1994, it is now the worlds' leading online shopping portal. He also holds stakes in Blue Origin and The Washington Post.

Name   : Elon Musk

Age   : 50

Fortune : $254 Billion

Requires: Being the co-founder and CEO of TESLA. With ownership stakes in Space Exploration Technologies, The Boring Company and Twitter.

Name   : Bernard Arnault

Age   : 73

Fortune : $145 Billion

Requires: Being the chair and CEO of LVMH. LVMH owns the Louis Vuitton, Hennessey, Marc Jacobs and Sephora brands. His wealth also lies in being a stake-holder in Christian Dior and Hermes.

Name   : Gautam Adan

Age   : 60

Fortune : $123 Billion

Requirements: Being the founder of Adani Group in Asia. He holds stakes in major Power, Transmissions, Gas and Green Energy companies in India. He created Adani Enterprises in 1988 to import and export goods, he then entered the power generation market in 2009 with Adani Power.

Name   : Larry Page

Age   : 49

Fortune : $106 Billion

Requires: Specialized skills. Another technical billionaire and it started in his college dorm room. In 1995 Larry and his friend Sergey came up with the idea of improving data extraction, devising a search engine. In 1998, they co-founded GOOGLE, under the company Alphabet.

Name   : Sergey Brin

Age   : 48

Fortune : $102 Billion

Requires: Specialized skills. Co-founder of GOOGLE. Stake-holder in Alphabet.

Name   : Larry Ellison

Age   : 77

Fortune : $96.1 Billion

Requires: Specialized Skills as a Computer programmer and moving on to research and development. He is the co-founder, Chair and CTO of Oracle (ORCL).

Note the dates when they started their businesses, and the current *ages* of the above personalities. This proves that they *did not become wealthy overnight.* The common aspect amongst them as well, is that they worked, they used their skill, and they put their ideas into the market and it performed well, very well! Their trick, was no trick at all, they were skilled, they were creative in their thinking, and they took the leap of starting up a business, *they faced many challenges but they persevered.*

The truth is*: **THERE IS NO SUCH THING AS EASY MONEY! QUICK BUCKS! OR***

FAST FINANCES! The only thing about money is that it is easy to spend and escapes very quickly from your bank account, right? Well, this is what I found really works, and it took quite a lot of disappointments and trial and error and hard work, before I got it right...

Here's what YOU NEED TO DO next:

i) **Be positive.** Take out a note-pad or pull out your laptop. Write down a few ideas that you may have. It should resemble something like this:

Ideas, Notes, Dreams and Ambitions

Ideas:	*Resources Available:*
Bake and sell	baking ingredients, baking equipment, electricity
Design Posters	computer, phone, design applications, internet access, printer
Offer local deliveries	vehicle, fuel, phone, map, experience
Tutor School kids	computer/phone, internet access, skills in math, science or languages

ii) **Be innovative.** Think about something that you would like to invent or produce or manufacture, and put it down on paper. If your idea is based on something someone else is already doing but you see room for improvement, go for it!

iii) **Don't just stop at 1 idea**, jot down at least five to ten ideas or plans, if you have one hundred ideas, that's ok too!

iv) **Use the resources you have** available around you. Try to start with ideas which don't need money to make money. Do projects for school kids or business plans for clients or designing a poster with a phrase which you can upload and sell (e.g., You can do this with an android phone or a computer). If you love baking and you have the ingredients, try to sell cupcakes to neighbors or to your local school. So instead of:

Image 1 ,

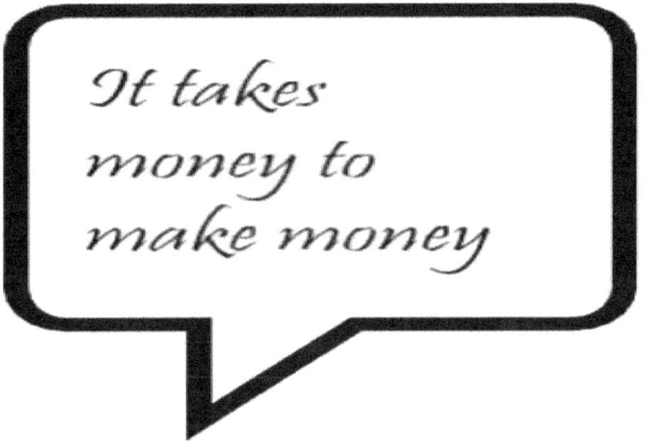

Your skills should improve and now your design should look more like:

Image2

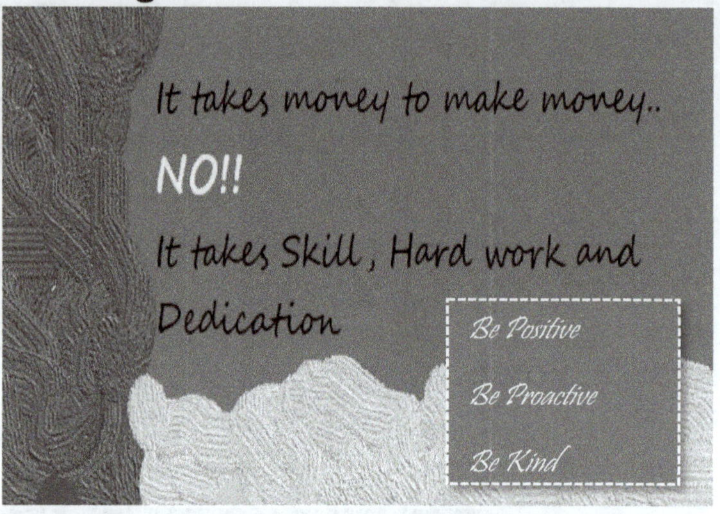

v) **Do a trial run** to get the feel of the global market. Put your idea out there, advertise it, even if it's not perfect yet. Listen to the customers, take the criticism, improve on your product.

vi) **Never lose heart.** Keep the positivity flowing. You are your biggest, and probably only, supporter right now.

vii) **Be proactive**. Set up a goal chart, with cut-off dates and figures. Paste it up on your wall, where you can see it. Revise your plans and tick them off as you accomplish your tasks each day. Something similar to this, but a little more exciting:

viii) **Balance** between being professional with your work but casual and easy in your attitude.

ix) **Do a lot of research** on all your plans/ goals/ ideas. Do not come across as a chancer, or as someone who does not know what they are doing, because you will lose the trust of potential customers and clients.

x) **Learn** a new skill which will boost your plan/idea. There are many free courses out there, choose one which will benefit your potential business, for e.g., a free social platform marketing course. Some courses require a minimal fee, and *only if you have the extra cash*, sign up for it.

xi)   **Start** developing a business plan.

xii) **Now that your skills have improved**, start on the manufacturing/production process.

xiii) **Start uploading and selling** your idea/product. Market your product again, this time with a better understanding of what customers want and need. Make sure you have good marketing exposure on as many advertising platforms as possible. YouTube, Instagram, TikTok and Facebook. (Try to gct in on the free advertising).

xiv) **Do not lose hope** if the sales are a bit slow at first. Move on to your next idea or plan and start working on it, and put it up for sale as well. Continue to do this until your item or idea starts to gain momentum. You will now gain customers and popularity. You are now well on your way to success.

xv)   **Be Kind. Be generous and helpful** to those in need (offer skills, ideas, food hampers, etc.). Do not become arrogant, do not forget your struggles and where you started.

xvi)   **Be Honest.** If you sell a product, make sure it is of good quality. Be truthful, if you have to deliver on a particular date and you cannot do it, be honest, you will gain respect, news will spread, and you will get more customers in this manner.

xvii) **BUT before you start, PRAY**, because nothing works without the **Will of the Almighty**. All the wealth in the world, each human being, every animal, every part of the universe and all that is in the heavens, belongs to Him, and only He can give you a portion of His treasures or deprive you of it.

I WISH YOU TONS OF SUCCESS IN YOUR BUSINESS!!

About The Author Zacharia G:

I have spent many years in Construction, Law and Finance Companies, together with studies and experience in Psychology, Law, Project Management, Education, Training, Skills and Development, amongst others. My Education has always been within British-based Institutions; hence my English is not quite American.

My overall objective is to inform and educate nations so that they can be productive, and make an effort towards self-development and lead a gratifying existence.